MANAGING YOUR EMOTIONS

RENEW & RESTORE BIBLE STUDIES

Finding Freedom from Anxiety and Stress

Managing Your Emotions

RENEW & RESTORE BIBLE STUDIES

Managing *your* Emotions

BY

CHRISTA KINDE

THOMAS NELSON
Since 1798

CONTENTS

Introduction   vii

SESSION 1:   A BUNDLE OF EMOTIONS   1

SESSION 2:   HAPPINESS AT ANY COST   9

SESSION 3:   TEMPER, TEMPER   17

SESSION 4:   THE GREEN-EYED MONSTER   25

SESSION 5:   LONELY HEARTS   33

SESSION 6:   WORRIES AND FEARS   41

SESSION 7:   THE DOLDRUMS   49

SESSION 8:   SCATTERED   57

SESSION 9:   MARY, MARY, QUITE CONTRARY   63

SESSION 10: PMSING   71

SESSION 11: MIXED-UP EMOTIONS   79

SESSION 12: KNOW THYSELF   87

Leader's Guide   95

INTRODUCTION

Why do you let your emotions take over,
lashing out and spitting fire?
Job 15:12 MSG

As children, we learn the ability to read faces. A smiling face means a person is happy. A frowning face means someone is sad. Simple, right?

Well, no, not really. Life is more complex than that. Our feelings don't just range between glad and sad. There are also feelings of anger, disappointment, fear, depression, loneliness, elation, awe, eagerness, longing, resentment, worry, grief, confusion, compassion, frustration, jealousy, guilt, ambition, pride, admiration, curiosity, and love—and that's just to name a few! What's more, our emotions rarely fit into just one of those categories. We usually have mixed emotions, conflicting emotions, or we jump from one to the other in a matter of moments. It can often feel exhausting and overwhelming—add those two to the list!

Most of us live at the mercy of our moods and emotions. We can't control what we feel. We just feel. But God says we are wise if we learn to manage our reactions to people and circumstances and determine how much our emotions will influence our lives.

Now, we're not here to deal with the really severe emotional disorders. They certainly exist and deserve attention, but we'll leave that to the experts. What we're going to tackle in this study are the garden-variety moods and emotions we deal with every day. We all struggle with our tempers. We all know what it's like to be jealous, lonely, worried, and overwhelmed. We all battle with rebellious feelings, not wanting to do what God asks of us. It's part of being human. Isn't it nice to know you're not alone?

THE PURPOSE OF THIS SERIES

The *Renew & Restore Bible Studies* are designed to help you connect with God through his Word, give Him your burdens and troubles, and experience the healing power of His promises. Whether you are studying individually or with a group, this book will give you the chance to reflect on key Scripture passages and consider how they apply to your life and circumstances. So pull out your Bible and a pen, and get ready to enter into quiet time with God.

FOR LEADERS

If you are leading a group through this study guide or engaging in individual study, please see the Leader's Guide at the back of the book for suggested answers and insights to the reflection questions.

A BUNDLE OF EMOTIONS

"A good man out of the good treasure of his heart
brings forth good; and an evil man out of the
evil treasure of his heart brings forth evil."
LUKE 6:45 NKJV

When we start talking about moods and emotions, we must begin with the heart. I guess you could say it's the heart of the matter! We call it the seat of our emotions, and we try to explain our feelings by referring to it. People can be described as hardhearted, softhearted, openhearted, warmhearted, coldhearted, fainthearted, or even heartless. Some people wear their heart on their sleeve. We can do something to our heart's content. We know what it's like to lose heart, take heart, have our heart set on something, have a change of heart, and have our hearts skip a beat. We can be heavyhearted, halfhearted, or lighthearted.

A story can be heartwarming, heart wrenching, or heartening. We can learn something by heart, have our hearts in the right place, and win the hearts of others. Some days, we don't have the heart to face our work. Other days, we tackle the job heartily, going at it heart and soul.

With all these words and phrases connecting our emotions to our hearts, one of our most important organs, it isn't surprising that our emotions play such an important role in our lives. And with so many different things going on within our hearts, it's no wonder our emotions get tangled up sometimes!

1. *The Bible talks a lot about the heart, and the emotions tangled up within it. God knows we all have our ups and downs. What two emotional extremes are mentioned in Proverbs 15:13?*

2. *What kinds of things are going on in our hearts, according to Proverbs 16:9? What can we take away from this passage?*

_____

_____

_____

_____

_____

_____

3. *The psalms are wonderful for giving us glimpses into the inner turmoil of the heart. Read Psalm 25:17 and Psalm 109:22. Can you relate to what David is experiencing?*

_____

_____

_____

_____

_____

We are moody people, as changeable as the weather. And because we're all so experienced in emotions, we know how to spot them. We can read faces. We can interpret body language. Often, our attitudes and moods come across loud and clear. Though we might try to hide our inner turmoil, our emotions leak out when we're with other people. Whether we realize it or not, we are being defined by the emotion we display most consistently. Throughout this study, we'll examine a range of different emotions we all experience and learn how we can better control these emotions, so they don't end up controlling us!

4. *When we allow our feelings—like worry, fear, and doubt—to carry us along, how does James 1:6 describe us?*

_____

_____

_____

_____

5. *Jesus never allowed His feelings to lead Him into sin. Still, it's a comfort to know the Lord completely understands how we feel. How does Hebrews 4:14–15 describe Jesus' inner struggles while on earth?*

_____

_____

_____

6. *Our moods, emotions, feelings, and attitudes are powerful and can easily overrule what we know is right. What advice does Paul give in Colossians 3:16 on how to counteract the tugging of our hearts?*

Digging Deeper

The Scriptures are filled with descriptions of our hearts. Have you ever noticed the wide variety of adjectives they use to describe it—both good and bad? Let's take a few minutes to dive deeper into some of these passages that describe the attitudes found in our hearts. If you are in a group or own multiple Bible translations, examine how different translations add new meaning to the text. Which of these passages stand out to you and why?

- Psalm 112:7
- Psalm 119:80
- Psalm 119:161
- Proverbs 16:5
- Proverbs 17:22
- Luke 8:15

PONDER & PRAY

In the days ahead, take time to ponder what is in your heart. Ask the Lord for a measure of detachment, so you can see the feelings that flit through your heart, the moods that shape your day, and the emotions that get the better of you. Tell the Lord what you discover and ask for His guidance. Then, take some Scripture—perhaps some of this week's verses—and plant them in your heart. The heart is not easily swayed if it is the dwelling place of the powerful Word of God.

Additional Notes & Prayer Requests

HAPPINESS AT ANY COST

He who is of a merry heart has a continual feast.
PROVERBS 15:15 NKJV

Though dozens of moods are available to us, one feeling is esteemed above all the others—happiness. We don't really mind what God has planned for us, so long as it brings us happiness. And what makes us happy? When things go our way. When everything runs smoothly in the direction we hoped it would go. No bumps. No interruptions. No obstacles. In order to maintain our happiness, we begin to avoid situations that might endanger it.

I want no regrets, so I will take no chances. I don't want to be disappointed, so I'll lower my expectations. I want to avoid embarrassment, so I will avoid speaking up. I don't want to experience sadness, so I will not allow myself to care. We set up emotional comfort zones and stay within

9

them. We create our own happy, little bubble—a safe haven, untouched by others. No one can make us budge, not even the Lord.

1. *The world tells us that following our hearts will lead to happiness. But what does Jeremiah tell us about the human heart in Jeremiah 17:9?*

_____

_____

_____

_____

2. *Solomon was wise, even in matters of the heart. What does he say about our hearts in Proverbs 28:26?*

_____

_____

_____

_____

3. *Our emotions can deceive us. Our own selfish desires can overrule what our heads tell us is right. What does Deuteronomy 11:16 warn?*

_____

_____

_____

_____

"I just want to be happy." That's not so bad, right? Or is it? When we place our own happiness as the highest goal in life, we do so at a great cost. We decide our happiness is more important than anyone else's. This self-centeredness begins to skew our perceptions. We begin to think that everything—including people—should fall in line with our expectations. If we are not happy, then things need to change. It's all about me—my plan, my choice, my comfort, and my happiness. We turn a blind eye to what other people are going through.

What's worse, our happiness becomes more important than God's truth. The things He asks of us in the Scriptures might just compromise our ultimate happiness. So we convince ourselves instead that God would want us to be happy, and we pick and choose the parts of the Bible we'll apply. We try to fit the Scriptures into our comfort zones. That's modular faith, not real faith. As Christians, we have to be willing to set aside our own personal happiness and focus instead on what God wants for our lives. It just might make us happier than we ever thought possible!

4. *God knows your heart. So why not give it to Him? What does Proverbs 3:5 tell us to do—and not to do?*

_____

_____

_____

_____

_____

5. *If we truly want God's help in achieving lasting happiness, He asks us to do . . . what? Check out Psalm 34:18.*

_____

_____

_____

_____

HAPPINESS AT ANY COST

6. *Happiness should never be our ultimate goal. Rather, we should be looking for God to make us new and give us a pure heart. What does God promise in Ezekiel 36:26?*

_____

_____

_____

_____

_____

_____

DIGGING DEEPER

There are lots of verses in the Bible that talk about God giving us a new heart, a clean heart, a joyful heart. When we allow our hearts to be stirred to do that which is good and right and useful to the Lord, God promises we'll find a happiness unlike any we've ever known. Take some time to explore the following verses and think about how you can apply them to your own life. Discuss with your study group, if you're a part of one.

- Psalm 19:14
- Psalm 51:10
- Psalm 119:1–3
- Ezekiel 18:31

PONDER & PRAY

This week, pray for God to help you understand the desires of your own heart. Then, when you sense your emotions are about to lead you into trouble, ask for the courage to stop following your heart everywhere it goes. Give up the impulse to put your happiness first, and place your trust in God and His Word instead. Depend on God to give you a new heart, one that is ready to do His will.

Additional Notes & Prayer Requests

_____

_____

_____

_____

_____

_____

_____

_____

_____

_____

_____

TEMPER, TEMPER

Better to dwell in the wilderness,
Than with a contentious and angry woman.
PROVERBS 21:19 NKJV

Anger has a lot of fiery connotations, doesn't it? We say tempers flare. Anger smolders in our hearts. We harbor burning wrath, seething emotions. We say someone's a hothead or that they have a short fuse. And when we can't contain our anger any longer, we blow our top and sparks fly.

There are lots of ways to vent our anger. We grit our teeth. We give someone The Look. We pull our hair, stamp our feet, say hateful things. But most of us are taught at an early age that temper tantrums are not acceptable. We're encouraged to exercise a little self-control. We're told to think before we speak, cool down, count to ten, and find healthy ways to express our frustration.

But some of us never learn to control our tempers. It's one of the most unmanageable moods we face. All too often, even the littlest things set us off, and we explode before we even think about what we're doing. When we do and say things in the heat of the moment, we can inflict a lot of damage. Anger unleashed almost always leads to feelings of regret.

1. *How does Proverbs 29:22 characterize an angry person?*

_____

_____

_____

_____

2. *What does Proverbs 14:29 tell us about people who cannot control their tempers?*

_____

_____

_____

_____

3. *We're far from alone in our struggles with our tempers. Many people in the Bible said words in the heat of the moment and behaved in ways they would later regret. Jonah is a prime example of this. Read Jonah chapter 4. How does God react to Jonah's temper tantrum?*

_____

_____

_____

_____

_____

Have you ever stopped to think about why we get angry? What's at the root of our temper? It's easiest to discern the heart of the matter with young children. They pitch a fit when they want something and we tell them "no." They howl when it's time to go home, because they'd rather continue having fun. They scream and cry when they want their own way. It's selfishness, plain and simple.

Are we so different? We get angry when we are inconvenienced. We get upset when we are disappointed, frustrated, and impatient. We lose our temper when our children disobey us (when we don't get our way). Some of us get into the habit of anger because we've learned it's the fastest way to get what we want. We're still losing our temper for selfish reasons, even as adults.

4. *How do we keep our anger from getting the better of us? Take a look at Psalm 37:8, Ephesians 4:31, and Colossians 3:8. What words are used for dealing with anger in each of them?*

_____

_____

_____

_____

_____

_____

5. *So does that mean we can never be angry—that all anger is a sin? Well, no. Let's look at what Psalm 4:4 says.*

_____

_____

_____

_____

_____

6. *It's impossible to say, "I will never be angry again." We need to set a realistic goal for ourselves. In Nehemiah 9:17, one of God's character traits is being "slow to anger." That's the ticket! What does Proverbs 16:32 say about a person who is slow to anger?*

DIGGING DEEPER

The Bible is full of wisdom and practical advice when it comes to anger. Here are several passages that offer us some much-needed insights. If you own multiple translations or are part of a small group, look at how different Bible translations offer new nuances. Is there a particular verse that resonates with you?

- Proverbs 15:1
- Proverbs 15:18
- Proverbs 19:11
- Proverbs 22:24
- Ephesians 4:26

PONDER & PRAY

When we delve into the moods and emotions that influence our lives, anger is easy to spot. But it can be very difficult to let go of! Still, it's important for us to learn how to keep our temper in check; none of us want to say or do things that we'll live to regret. This week, pray for God's mercy and guidance as you address the anger harbored in your heart. Ask the Lord to make you more like Him—slow to anger and full of mercy.

ADDITIONAL NOTES &
PRAYER REQUESTS

SESSION 4

THE GREEN-EYED MONSTER

Wrath is cruel and anger a torrent,
But who is able to stand before jealousy?
PROVERBS 27:4 NKJV

Even though children are very different from one another, they are all very concerned with equality. If one child receives an apple, they all expect apples. Pies and pizzas must be divided with precision, so no one has a bigger piece than anyone else. The worst complaint they can bring against each other is the resentful wail that "It's not fair!"

Of course, we know very well the root of their obsession is *not* a desire for justice. Far from it! They're nitpicking and weighing and comparing everything that comes their way because they are greedy at heart and jealous of one another. It sounds terrible, but it's part of human nature.

Jealousy—it's the green-eyed monster. Solomon says, "Anger is cruel, and wrath is like a flood, but jealousy is even more dangerous" (Proverbs

27:4 NLT). It's an emotion that doesn't fade away when we grow up. We still have an urge to say, "It's not fair!" when life doesn't give us what we think we deserve.

Even Christians are susceptible to pangs of jealousy. We are green with envy when it seems God has blessed other people more than us. We resent this one's bigger house or that one's new car. We wonder why some people are smarter, prettier, *better* than us. Instead of appreciating what we have and thanking God for the blessings He's given us, we focus on the things that others have that we lack. Such foolishness!

1. *Envy is like a disease. How does Solomon say it affects us in Proverbs 14:30?*

2. Covetousness is such a danger to our hearts that God included it in the Ten Commandments. "You shall not covet your neighbor's house; you shall not covet your neighbor's wife, nor his male servant, nor his female servant, nor his ox, nor his donkey, nor anything that is your neighbor's" (Exodus 20:17). What is the consequence of covetousness, according to Proverbs 15:27?

_____

_____

_____

_____

3. What does Psalm 119:36 say is the alternative to covetousness?

_____

_____

_____

_____

_____

4. *Paul knew a thing or two about sidestepping jealousy. What advice does he give in 1 Corinthians 10:24 and Philippians 2:4?*

_____

_____

_____

_____

_____

_____

_____

As Christians, we are told to love one another. Jesus, Paul, Peter, Matthew, Mark, Luke, John, and James—they all say the same thing. "I did not come to be served, but to serve." "Love your neighbor as yourself." "Consider one another." "Giving preference to one another." These are the noble ideals that we should pursue.

But at some point, don't you feel the urge to shout, "Hey! What about me? How do I know my needs will be taken care of?" If we're spending so much time being self-sacrificing, won't people just walk all over us? Won't we be taken for granted?

It's only after I've exhausted myself with indignation and jealousy that I realize something: everyone feels this way. We all believe our efforts go unnoticed. We all struggle to put others before ourselves. And that's when I pray, *God, give me a servant's heart, because I want to be like You. And I know You see my efforts, even when no one else does.*

5. *You have to love Martha! There's someone who wasn't afraid to march into a room full of people (who were just sitting around until supper was ready) and say what we've all felt at one time or another: "Hey! What about me?" What does she say to Jesus in Luke 10:40, and how does He respond?*

6. *Let's examine the practical advice Paul has for us in Galatians 6:4–5. What do you take away from this passage?*

7. *We should never allow the green-eyed monster of jealousy to cause our eyes to wander from the task God has set before us. We each must answer for ourselves before the Lord. What does Paul say about this in 1 Corinthians 3:8?*

DIGGING DEEPER

Some sins seem harmless enough. Who cares if we envy someone else? Nobody can see it. Nobody will know. But the greed we hide reveals a heart that is self-seeking, ungrateful, and covetous. God sees. God knows. And He takes these things very seriously. Just look at the sins that are ranked right next to greed and envy in the Scriptures. How do you feel after reading these lists?

- Mark 7:21–22
- 1 Corinthians 5:10–11
- 1 Corinthians 6:10
- Ephesians 5:5
- 1 Peter 2:1–2

PONDER & PRAY

This week, let's work to banish the green-eyed monster from our hearts. Jealousy, envy, covetousness, greed, resentment—have they played a prominent role in your mood lately? Remind yourself that you will only have the Lord to answer to in the end—same as everybody else. Pray for God to help you quench the urge to compare. Ask for a generous spirit. Ask for a pure servant's heart.

ADDITIONAL NOTES & PRAYER REQUESTS

SESSION 5

LONELY HEARTS

"Lo, I am with you always, even to the end of the age."
MATTHEW 28:20 NKJV

When we moved a few years ago, it didn't take us very long to find a new church home. What did take a while, though, was fitting in. At our previous church, everyone knew us. We had shared experiences. We had shared laughter and tears. We had known our niche in the congregation. Starting over was hard. Nobody knew our story. Nobody knew our gifts. Nobody knew our talents, skills, likes and dislikes. And because nobody knew us, we felt like nobodies.

Over the first several months of settling in, I struggled with loneliness. It wasn't homesickness. I didn't yearn to go back to where we had been. It was a loneliness to know and be known. I wanted to put names to all the faces in the crowd and have them know my name too. I wanted my pastor to know how much I respected him and that I was taking his sermons to heart. I wanted the women in the kitchen to know I enjoyed baking and would love to help out. I wanted people to find out what I was like and to *be* liked.

1. *David describes the loneliness we often feel in Psalm 69:20. Why does he wish he had someone to talk to?*

2. *"I've known drudgery and hard labor, many a long and lonely night without sleep, many a missed meal, blasted by the cold, naked to the weather" (2 Corinthians 11:27 MSG). Paul knew loneliness. Does it seem strange that someone who was such a pillar of faith could feel this way?*

3. *In Genesis, God declared, "It is not good that man should be alone"
    (Genesis 2:18). God made us to need one another. What does
    Ecclesiastes 4:9–11 say one friend can do for another? Have you
    experienced this in your own life?*

---

4. *There are those of us who are alone most of the time. Paul uses the
    example of the widow. What does 1 Timothy 5:5 say this lonely
    woman can do?*

How do you cultivate a friendship? It isn't always easy. First, you have to find someone who wants a good friend. That can be a challenge in and of itself! Then, you have to find out about each other—personality, background, beliefs, likes, trustworthiness. Let's face it, we don't always click with each other. It takes a lot of time to really bond, but over the course of months and years, friendship grows. Before you know it, you are giggling over private jokes, finishing each other's sentences, and checking in with each other regularly.

We believers are offered this kind of close bond as well. Jesus called His disciples "friends," and He extends to us the same invitation. Have you ever considered sharing things with the Lord you'd normally tell a friend? Have you pursued your Savior through the Scriptures so that you know Him better than anyone else? Wouldn't it be wonderful to leave loneliness behind forever, knowing that God is always near, always faithful, and always ready to listen?

5. *Our hearts yearn to know and be known, and there are times when we just need to get some things off our chest. We need an understanding ear to listen as we pour out our hearts. When times like that come, what does David say to do in Psalm 62:8?*

6. *During His three years of ministry on the earth, Jesus didn't try to go it alone. He surrounded Himself with disciples and friends. Yet look at John 16:32. When the disciples abandoned Him, did He feel alone? What was Christ's attitude?*

DIGGING DEEPER

No matter how lonely we feel at times, God is always with us. Yet it can be difficult to remember that in the midst of our sadness. Let's review the following Scriptures to remind ourselves that God is there to listen, that He cares about our troubles, and that He wants to fill us with His grace, peace, and love. Which of these verses do you find the most comforting? Discuss with your small group if you're a part of one.

- 2 Corinthians 13:11
- 2 Thessalonians 3:16
- John 14:16–17
- Colossians 2:5
- 2 John 1:3
- Matthew 28:20

PONDER & PRAY

If you find yourself feeling lonely in the days ahead, ask the Lord to help you to grasp Whose you are, Who goes with you, and the gifts that abide with you because of that. Work to cultivate your friendship with Him, and He will lift your heart out of loneliness. Thank God for the blessings of friendship, and look for ways to reach out to others this week. Be that listening ear, be the one with the encouraging word, be the one to hear and know and understand.

ADDITIONAL NOTES &
PRAYER REQUESTS

SESSION 6

WORRIES
AND FEARS

"Do not fret—it only causes harm."
PSALM 37:8 NKJV

When I take life one day at a time, things seem relatively manageable. But more often than not, my mind stretches forward, and I begin to worry about my tomorrows. What if my new boss is a tyrant? What if I forget to pay the bills this week? What if it rains during the kids' soccer game? What if the house burns down? Do we have enough life insurance? What if I lose my job? What if it's cancer? Am I a good parent? Will we ever have enough money to retire?

Sure, we need to plan ahead, but we shouldn't go borrowing trouble. If we allow our stomachs to roil over all the possibilities the future may hold, we'll make ourselves sick. Jesus wasn't kidding when He said that today has enough worries of its own! But how do we quit fretting about the future when it comes so naturally?

1. *We may be tempted to hide our troubles, to pretend that everything's fine, but what does David invite God to do in Psalm 139:23?*

_____

_____

_____

_____

2. *And what can we do when we are afraid, according to Psalm 56:3?*

_____

_____

_____

_____

3. *God assures us that we don't have to worry about the things of this world. What specific things are mentioned in Psalm 91:5 and Psalm 112:7?*

_____

_____

_____

_____

_____

_____

We've all encountered anxiety at some point in our lives. Even the most carefree person knows what anxiety feels like. It's wondering what might happen. It's knowing things are out of our hands. It's losing control. It's expecting the worst. It's having the jitters. Queasiness. Sweating palms. Trembling hands. Pounding heart. Shortness of breath. Loss of appetite.

When worry, anxiety, fretting, and fear overwhelm our hearts and minds, we tend to forget everything else. But God wants us to remember one very important thing in the chaos—Him. When fears press in around you, cling to God. Hang onto His promises for you. Hold tight to hope. Trust God with your very life, and your faith will drive out the fears.

43

4. Psalm 37:7 says, "Don't worry about evil people who prosper or fret about their wicked schemes" (NLT). What attitude should we cling to instead, according to Psalm 56:4?

_____

_____

_____

_____

_____

5. Jesus has some practical advice for us when we're feeling anxious or worried. Look at Matthew 6:25–27.

_____

_____

_____

_____

_____

6. *When Jesus departed from this earth, He left us a gift. What is that gift, according to John 14:27?*

DIGGING DEEPER

Though we may guard against it, sometimes our hearts are clutched by fear. God doesn't want us to be ruled by fear, but to trust in Him for all we need. Jesus said to His disciples, "Let not your heart be troubled; you believe in God, believe also in Me" (John 14:1). Trusting Jesus and holding on to God's promises can do much to dispel our fears. Let's look at just a few more of the verses in the New Testament that urge us to hold fast:

- Philippians 3:12
- 1 Thessalonians 5:21
- 1 Timothy 6:19
- 2 Timothy 1:13
- Hebrews 3:6
- Hebrews 10:23

PONDER & PRAY

Use your prayer time this week to bring your anxiety before the Lord. Ask Him to guide you along the path of peace. Then, search the Scriptures for the various promises God has made to you as a believer. Every time you begin to worry, recall one of these precious promises. Then trust God to keep His word.

Additional Notes & Prayer Requests

THE DOLDRUMS

*We dry up like autumn leaves—
sin-dried, we're blown off by the wind.*
ISAIAH 64:6 MSG

Sometimes we just feel stuck. It's like we're on an ancient ship in the middle of a perfectly still sea. There's no wind to move us forward, no currents to drift us along. We feel restless, but oddly listless as well. The captain paces, stopping periodically to squint up into the sky. It's the dreaded doldrums. And the only thing you can do is wait for them to pass.

In every Christian's life, there are dry spells, times of dullness, seasons of waiting. Often, the doldrums come when we've gotten burnt out, when we have nothing left to give. Spiritual exhaustion leaves us uncaring, listless, and longing for something to change. The doldrums aren't as severe as depression, and yet it feels as though we'll never snap out of it. Like we'll never be excited or energized again.

One of the hardest things the Lord asks us to do is wait. We would rather have things happen now so we can keep moving. But God finds periods of waiting on Him are very beneficial. Still, just because we know something is good for us, doesn't mean we like it! How do we wait on the Lord when the waiting feels awful?

1. *Have you ever felt spiritually stranded? Have you had that "blah" mood descend and found it impossible to shake? David shares his misery in Psalm 6:6. How does he describe it?*

2. *Dry seasons come, even to those who love God. What brings on the dryness, according to Proverbs 17:22? Is it possible that this is what's happened to you?*

3. *Another word to describe life's doldrums is a feeling of dullness. Why do people grow dull, according to Acts 28:27?*

_____

_____

_____

_____

_____

_____

4. *Even in a period of waiting, there is help for us while we wait. What does Romans 8:26 encourage us with?*

_____

_____

_____

_____

_____

I love plants. My home and office wouldn't seem quite the same without green things scattered about. I've had ivies, ferns, gardenias, lemon trees, peace plants, and many others. Over the years I've had varying degrees of success with these plants, mainly because I sometimes forget to water them. Now, a plant can get along okay without spritzing and dusting and fertilizing, but when you forget to water it, it just shrivels up and dies. That's it. The end.

That's why most of the plants I keep now are philodendrons. They're virtually indestructible. You can forget to water them for a week, and they'll bounce right back. They take my absentmindedness in stride.

Sometimes, I think my heart is like a philodendron, because I don't always take good care of it. It gets dusty with disuse. I forget to feed it. Worse, I withhold it from God, and it suffers times of drought. It wilts and shrivels. But whenever I come to my senses and return to the Lord, my heart is soaked in living water. And it revives.

5. God "energizes those who get tired" (Isaiah 40:29 MSG) and "rekindles burned-out lives with fresh hope" (1 Samuel 2:8 MSG). What does Jeremiah 31:25 say that God can do? What does Jesus offer to those who are weary in Matthew 11:28–30?

6. *No matter how long you seem to be stuck in the doldrums, don't lose faith in God's ability to answer and refresh. Why does David say he never lost heart, according to Psalm 27:13?*

DIGGING DEEPER

When we're stuck in a dry spell, the best thing we can do while we wait is draw closer to God. One of the words Jesus often uses is "Come." It is a word of invitation. The Lord wants us to be close to Him. He calls to us and asks us to follow Him. The following verses will help us understand what that means. If you're part of a study group or own multiple translations of the Bible, look at how the wording changes between translations. What new meanings can you glean from them?

- Matthew 19:21
- Luke 19:5
- Matthew 19:14
- John 6:37
- John 7:37

Ponder & Pray

Are you in a season of dryness? Do you feel as if you're stranded in your spiritual walk and you long to move forward? Fill your prayers this week with pleas for refreshment, revitalization, and revival. Turn to Him daily for the strength and life only He can supply. Ask God to stir your heart, to stir up your hunger for His Word, to stir up your thirst for righteousness.

Additional Notes and Prayer Requests

SESSION 8

SCATTERED

My spirit is overwhelmed within me;
My heart within me is distressed.
PSALM 143:4 NKJV

We all know what it means to scatter something. Lots of things are easily scattered: papers, leaves, confetti, thoughts. Anyone who's tried to keep a house clean and orderly knows it's easier said than done—it's like it *wants* to be cluttered and jumbled. These days, there are so many demands on our time that if we're not careful, we start to feel jumbled too.

When we're pulled in too many different directions, we barely have time to think. Our schedules are packed. We are spread too thin. We're running in circles. Life becomes a flurry of activity, all hustle and bustle with no moment to catch a breath. The sheer number of our responsibilities is oppressive. We are overactive, overcommitted, overwhelmed. When we're this busy, we only have time to give a dab of effort here and there; we don't have time to dive down deep and make any real progress. At times like these, we are easily confused, easily distracted, easily led astray. All our self-control is scattered to the wind.

1. *How did Job describe his emotional response to the troubles he was facing in Job 30:27?*

_____

_____

_____

2. *We probably don't use the term "scattered" too often when we're talking about our emotions, but we frequently use the word "overwhelmed." David said, "My spirit was overwhelmed within me" (Psalm 142:3). How does he express the feelings in his heart in Psalm 38:8?*

_____

_____

_____

_____

So what are we supposed to do when we're feeling scattered and over-whelmed? Are we supposed to toughen up and keeping pushing until all our ducks are finally in a row—until our lives are more organized, neat, tidy, predictable? The world may answer that question with a resounding "yes," but as Christians, we know that we don't have to carry our burdens alone. God sees our struggles, and He wants to offer us a sense of peace and safety. The next time you're feeling scattered, don't try to pick up all the pieces as fast as you can. Instead, bring your burdens to God in prayer and ask Him to give you His healing Spirit.

3. *Take a look at the introduction to Psalm 102. How was David feeling at that moment? What does Psalm 102:1 say he did when he felt like this?*

_____

_____

_____

_____

4. *Take a look at Psalm 61:2. What does David ask God to do for him?*

_____

_____

_____

_____

5. *What is the psalmist's prayer in Psalm 86:11? How does this attitude guard against being scattered?*

_____

_____

_____

_____

_____

_____

6. *In order to avoid being scattered, our hearts must stay focused—have a purpose. What does David say about this in Psalm 84:5?*

_____

_____

_____

_____

_____

Digging Deeper

The busyness of our days is enough to scatter our hearts and leave us overwhelmed. It takes a measure of determination to keep our eyes steadily on our Savior and the path He has set before us. We want to be able to join David in saying, "My heart is steadfast, O God, my heart is steadfast" (Psalm 57:7). Let's look at a few more verses about steadfastness to inspire ourselves this week.

- Psalm 51:10
- 1 Corinthians 15:58
- Colossians 1:23
- Hebrews 3:14
- Hebrews 6:19

Ponder & Pray

We cannot allow our scattered emotions to overwhelm us. Like David, let's pray this week for the Lord to lead us to the higher rock. Ask Him to unite your heart, instead of letting its turmoil scatter you to the winds. Pray for an understanding of God's purpose for your life, so you can stop running in different directions and purposefully move forward in your spiritual journey.

Additional Notes & Prayer Requests

_____

_____

_____

_____

_____

_____

_____

_____

_____

_____

_____

_____

MARY, MARY, QUITE CONTRARY

Perverse minds are always cooking up something nasty,
always stirring up trouble.
PROVERBS 6:14 MSG

*P*erversity is not a term we often use nowadays. It's one of those obscure Bible words that has fallen out of everyday use. The dictionary defines perversity as "obstinately persisting in an error or fault," and "turning away from what is right and good." Other synonyms for perverse would be wayward, ungovernable, obstinate, and contradictory.

Contrary is another word we don't often hear, except in the nursery rhyme, "Mary, Mary, quite contrary, how does your garden grow?" It's definition? "Unwilling to accept guidance or advice." As sinners, we all have a tendency toward perversity and contrariness. Sometimes it seems that even though we know what the right thing to do is, we can't help but turn willfully away from it.

When you were a child, what was the fastest way to get you to do something? The tongue-in-cheek answer to that question: to forbid you from doing it. Our perversity is so ingrained in our hearts that even when we are little, we rebel against authority. It's the contrary streak that asks, "Why not?" and "What'll happen if I do?"

When we're adults, our rebelliousness finds other ways to show itself. We're reluctant to do what we know is right. We shut our ears to the prompting of the Spirit. We avoid the direction of the Scriptures. We try to be independent, self-sufficient. And we let our foul moods get the better of us, even though we know we shouldn't.

1. *Sometimes, when we run across a verse of Scripture that convicts us, we dig in our heels and resist the change we know needs to come. How does Proverbs 19:3 characterize such a person?*

_____

_____

_____

_____

_____

_____

2. *What does Proverbs 11:20 say about those who harbor perversity in their hearts?*

_____

_____

_____

_____

_____

_____

   Do you know someone who is very contrary? The minute someone tells them they have to do something, they don't want to do it. They hate to be told what they'll like, what they'll feel, or what they really ought to try. They go out of their way to be different from other people. They ignore people's suggestions or advice, preferring to come up with their own ideas and make up their own mind about things. I know someone like that—me! And what's really sad is I find it easy to excuse this flaw in my nature by pretending it's some kind of enviable character quality. I call it creativity or independence or self-sufficiency. In truth, I am rebellious and proud, contrary and perverse.

   Have you ever tried to justify some little deceitfulness in your heart by calling it something else? When God calls us to look into our hearts with honest eyes, we will undoubtedly find something we didn't want to see. We cannot ignore it or re-define it before God. We can only confess it and ask Him to help us overcome it.

3. *What is the reality of living contrary to God, and what is the result of clinging to our rebellious ways? Take a look at Isaiah's warning in Isaiah 30:13.*

---

4. *What is the consequence of an unrepentant heart, according to Romans 2:5?*

---

5. Look at Jeremiah's prayer of confession in Lamentations 1:20. Why
    has he been so troubled?

_____

_____

_____

_____

_____

6. King Hezekiah's prayer for the people of God was, "Do not be
    stubborn . . . but submit yourselves to the LORD" (2 Chronicles 30:8
    NLT). What does Hebrews 12:9 say about submitting to God?

_____

_____

_____

_____

_____

DIGGING DEEPER

Most of the time cheerful submission seems like an oxymoron. How could those two words possibly go together? We tend to think of submission as grudging, not joyful. But God knows our hearts, so when He calls us to obedience, He wants our heart to be in it. God wants us to cheerfully submit to His will. Take a look at these Scriptures that talk about cheer. What reasons do we have to be cheerful, according to God's Word? Write down your thoughts in the notes section at the end of this session.

- Matthew 9:2
- Matthew 9:22
- 2 Corinthians 9:7
- John 16:33

PONDER & PRAY

Has a contrary heart found you resisting what you know to be good and right and true? Does your quiet rebellion leave you feeling cranky and defensive with those around you? Pray this week for the courage to let go, to trust God, to be a willing follower. Pray for joy, so your submission will be cheerful. Pray for a teachable heart that will not turn away from wise counsel. Trust that God's way is the best, and control your contrariness by giving control over to Him.

ADDITIONAL NOTES AND PRAYER REQUESTS

_____

_____

_____

_____

_____

_____

_____

_____

_____

_____

_____

_____

PMSing

If you fall to pieces in a crisis,
there wasn't much to you in the first place.
PROVERBS 24:10 MSG

There's no use trying to deny it. For women, there is an ebb and flow to our emotions that corresponds to our monthly cycle. What's funny is that even though our moods tend to swing at the same pace every month, many of us never realize it's happening. We're too close to it—actually, we're right in the middle of it! From our perspective, the boss is just a bit bossier, the kids are just a bit more unruly, traffic is a bit more congested, your friends are a bit more exasperating, and everything in general has become very irritating. But those things haven't changed at all—we have!

For most of us, when "that time of the month" draws near, we get edgy, touchy, irritable, moody, and downright grumpy. Other women face the onset of their period with a different demeanor. They become

71

quiet, introspective, super-sensitive, and weepy. They feel guilty for things they didn't do and are hard on themselves for the things they did.

As difficult as it is to control our emotions on any given day, it feels impossible when our hormones are actively working against us. But we can't just throw in the towel and let our emotions take over. Moods, cycles, and PMS are unavoidable hurdles for women, so we may as well face them head on.

1. *We often hear how people reveal their true character when placed in a crisis situation. James 1:3 says, "You know that under pressure, your faith-life is forced into the open and shows its true colors" (MSG). When you undergo premenstrual pressures, how does your faith hold up?*

2. *Jesus said, "Those things which proceed out of the mouth come from the heart" (Matthew 15:18). Our words reveal what we hide inside. What is revealed by our words, according to Matthew 12:34–35?*

---

3. *Look at what Solomon said about women in Proverbs 14:1. Which of these women do you tend to be? What about when it's that time of the month?*

It's silly to pretend we're always skipping along under blue skies with a happy heart. There are days when we just don't feel like skipping. We don't feel like smiling. We don't feel like talking. We don't feel like working. We don't feel like cooking. And we certainly don't feel like putting any effort into being pleasant. Frankly, we'd really rather everyone just go away.

Unfortunately, we cannot pause life just because we're not in the mood for it. A woman's got to do what a woman's got to do, whether she feels like it or not. Those are times when we have to reach right down into that new heart of ours and find enough strength from the Lord to make it through the next day, the next hour, the next minute.

4. *Peter's first epistle tells us the "hidden person of the heart" is where the Lord's eyes are fixed (1 Peter 3:4). He is in the business of changing us from the inside out. Only He can give us the new heart we need. Ezekiel 36:26 says, "I'll give you a new heart, put a new spirit in you. I'll remove the stone heart from your body and replace it with a heart that's God-willed, not self-willed" (MSG). What's the difference between a heart that is God-willed and one that is self-willed?*

_____

_____

_____

_____

5. *What did Paul want to be revealed in his life, according to the first part of Galatians 1:16?*

---

6. *When we're tempted to start PMSing, we need to be wise. King Solomon says the beginning of wisdom is the fear of the Lord. And "a woman who fears the LORD, she shall be praised" (Proverbs 31:30). How do we fear God? Read Deuteronomy 10:12–13.*

DIGGING DEEPER

When we live a life characterized by the fear of the Lord, even the emotional ebb and flow of the month will not completely shake us from our firm footing in His Word. Instead, the Lord we serve will characterize our lives. We who serve Jesus will become like Him, and others will see Christ in us. Here are a few verses that talk about Christ in us to inspire you this week.

- 2 Corinthians 11:10
- 2 Corinthians 13:3
- 1 Timothy 1:16
- Galatians 2:20

PONDER & PRAY

Sometimes we need to be reminded of the seriousness with which God deals with sin. He doesn't accept excuses, even when we're PMSing. Remember the words of Isaiah: "The LORD of hosts, Him you shall hallow; Let Him be your fear, And let him be your dread" (Isaiah 8:13). This week, pray to the Lord to give you a God-willed heart. Ask Him to teach you the godly fear that will lead to eternal life. Then pray for the strength to become a woman who fears the Lord, not a foolish woman who is ruled by her emotions.

ADDITIONAL NOTES AND PRAYER REQUESTS

MIXED-UP EMOTIONS

Even in laughter the heart may sorrow,
And the end of mirth may be grief.
PROVERBS 14:13 NKJV

We've probably all had our share of mishaps behind the wheel of a car. Turning the wrong way down a one-way street. Bumping up over a curb so we're parked with one wheel on the sidewalk. Scraping the paint off the bumper when we pull too far into a parking spot. Just navigating on unfamiliar roads can be more of an adventure than we bargained for. We miss a street sign and have to backtrack. We get turned around. Even lost.

Mixed-up emotions are like mixed-up directions. We're trying to navigate life's highways, but we have feelings pulling us in different directions. We zip along, chasing after other peoples' expectations of us. We detour around situations that might make us feel guilty or uncomfortable. We get distracted by all the things that clamor for our attention until we forget which way we're going. We become lost and confused. We go astray.

1. *Our emotions can be good at multitasking, hitting us with several different feelings at once. When we find ourselves being tugged in different directions, what does Paul remind us in Ephesians 4:17–24?*

2. *When we're feeling lost, we often instinctively try to solve the problem ourselves instead of reaching out to God. What is the danger of going it alone, according to Proverbs 14:12?*

3. *God often refers to us as little lost sheep. He knows how much we need His guidance. How are our lives as lambs described in Isaiah 53:6 and Jeremiah 50:6?*

4. *When we feel turned around and confused by the clamoring of our moods and emotions, it's important to remember God won't let us stay lost. What promise are we given in Jeremiah 23:4?*

Our emotions are capable of an amazing progression. Early in our marriage, my husband headed out for an evening meeting. He'd been gone for a while, but I was sure he'd be home soon, so I sat up waiting for him. Hour after hour passed, and still no sound of the key in the door. While I paced through our home, my mood underwent some incredible shifts.

At first, I wasn't really concerned—I just thought the meeting was running late. But as the hours ticked by, I grew more and more worried. Did he have car trouble? An accident? Was he in the hospital? Then I started to get angry. Why hadn't he called? Didn't he know how scared I was? How could he do this to me? And when he finally pulled into the driveway, I was so relieved I almost cried.

Have you ever ridden that emotional roller coaster? It's hard to stay calm in the heat of the moment, but the next time you're feeling overwhelmed by mixed-up emotions, try not to rush around in a panic. Instead, call out to the Shepherd of your soul. He will come after you and lead you back to where you're supposed to be.

5. *If you could use some reassurance right now, look at Ezekiel 34:15–16. What does God say He will do?*

_____

_____

_____

_____

_____

6.   *God knows that we need a shepherd, and He gave us the best one we could ask for, His own Son. Look at how Jesus describes Himself in John 10:14–15.*

7.   *No matter how mixed-up we might become, God is there to lead us along when we seek Him. The psalms are filled with prayers asking God to take charge. What does Psalm 31:3 say?*

DIGGING DEEPER

When we're following our own path, it's easy to get mixed-up, confused, lost, and overwhelmed with emotion. We're much better off following God and entrusting our lives to His leading and care. God's way is a good way. Here are some more verses to inspire you to follow the Lord's path. If you're part of a study group or own multiple translations, look at the way different translations can add new context to the Scriptures. Which verses stand out to you?

- Psalm 16:11
- Psalm 25:5
- Psalm 119:35
- Psalm 119:105
- Psalm 143:10

PONDER & PRAY

This week you can talk to the Lord as a sheep to your Shepherd. Tell Him your concerns and confusion. Let Him know what's been on your mind lately. Ask Him for the strength, comfort, nourishment, and peace only He can provide. Remember, you don't need to know where He's going to take you. All you have to do is trust Him and follow Him. His is a good path.

ADDITIONAL NOTES &
PRAYER REQUESTS

SESSION 12

KNOW THYSELF

Help me understand, so I can keep your teachings,
obeying them with all my heart.
PSALM 119:34 NCV

Some days, our feelings seem out of control. We're reacting to everything that lands in front of us, and we feel like we just can't help it. Emotions are often compared to a roller coaster—dizzying heights, plunging depths, and unexpected turns. It's impossible to get rid of our emotions; like it or not, they're here to stay. So it's absolutely vital that we take the time to sort through all our emotions and try to understand them.

Solomon calls our heart the wellspring of life (Proverbs 4:23). It's the starting point of who we are, and it determines who we will become. That's why it's so important to pay attention to what's going on in there! We need to get to know ourselves, understand what's going on inside, be in touch with our emotions, know what makes us tick. God has given us all these emotions, and it's our job to be good stewards of them.

1. *It takes careful stewardship to manage our emotions and do the right thing. Jesus urges us to use righteous judgment in deciding what to do: "Use your head—and heart!—to discern what is right" (John 7:24 MSG). We all face choices, and we must keep a cool head and take care in the choosing. What choice did Joshua make in Joshua 24:15?*

_____

_____

_____

_____

2. *Doing the right thing may seem like a no-brainer, but when it comes down to the nitty-gritty of living, being good can be very hard! That's where careful stewardship needs to meet supernatural assistance. What does Psalm 105:4 say we should do?*

_____

_____

_____

_____

After everything we've talked about so far, it might seem as if our moods and emotions are a curse rather than a blessing. They give us so much trouble! What good are emotions if they only drive us crazy? But God has given us all these emotions for a very good reason. Think about it. Our emotions are what make us empathetic. We are able to put ourselves in another's place and understand instinctively how someone else is feeling. We are capable of great understanding, great compassion, and great mercy. Jesus urges His followers to love one another, care for one another, and encourage one another, and our emotions are what make us perfectly suited to do just that!

3. *Sometimes it seems like emotions are one of those "great things which we cannot comprehend" (Job 37:5). But they do serve a very important purpose. What wouldn't we be able to comprehend if we didn't have these emotions, according to Ephesians 3:17–19?*

---

4. *Emotions are gifts from God, but that doesn't mean we will automatically use them as we should. Just look at Paul—he battled with himself all the time. We will too. What was Peter's encouragement to those with gifts in 1 Peter 4:10?*

_____

_____

_____

_____

5. *Over and over, we are encouraged to trust God and do good. Instead of letting our emotions hamper us, we need to step out in faith and "just do it." What do Isaiah 1:17 and Hebrews 13:16 say about doing good?*

_____

_____

_____

_____

_____

6. *Doing good will prove to be a lifelong battle for us. We may gain great wisdom. We may show great faith. We may bear much fruit. But we'll never "arrive" here on this earth. Our guard will always have to be up, and our dependence on God must be complete. Does that sound like a long, exhausting fight? Paul knew it might seem so. What encouragement does he offer to all believers in Galatians 6:9?*

DIGGING DEEPER

When we depend on Christ for what we need, the Bible assures us that we can overcome anything—even our seemingly unmanageable emotions! Here are some verses that address both depending on God and overcoming adversity. In the additional notes section at the end of this session, make a note of the verses you can turn to the next time your emotions start to feel out of control.

- Deuteronomy 7:9
- Isaiah 26:3
- John 16:33
- Romans 12:21
- 1 John 4:4
- 1 John 5:4

PONDER & PRAY

As we close this study, pray that God will bring back to your mind all the lessons you have needed to hear. Pray especially for the discernment to know yourself and the determination to do good each and every day. Ask the Lord to show you all the ways He is faithful, and thereby strengthen your faith. Put your trust in Him, and depend on Him for help with your heart—the moods, emotions, and feelings He has given you. When we become good stewards of our hearts and learn to manage our emotions, we can use them for the good of others and for God's glory.

ADDITIONAL NOTES & PRAYER REQUESTS

LEADER'S
GUIDE

SESSION 1

1. "A merry heart makes a cheerful countenance, But by sorrow of the heart the spirit is broken" (Proverbs 15:13). When our hearts are light, we can't help but look and feel cheerful. But when we're sad, it can feel as though our very spirits are broken.

2. "A man's heart plans his way, But the LORD directs his steps" (Proverbs 16:9). Our hearts are filled with everything that makes us . . . us! Our feelings, our dreams, our commitments, our loyalties, our personality, and our plans. It's such a busy place, it's no wonder we find ourselves in so much turmoil! We can help to calm the turbulence by turning control over to God and letting Him direct our steps forward.

3. "The troubles of my heart have enlarged; Bring me out of my distresses" (Psalm 25:17). Often when we're distressed or overwhelmed, our troubles seem to grow and grow until they fill our minds. "I am poor and needy, And my heart is wounded within me" (Psalm 109:22). We can take comfort in the knowledge that even in our darkest hours, God can heal our wounded hearts.

4. "He who doubts is like a wave of the sea, driven and tossed by the wind" (James 1:6). This isn't the only time this imagery is used to describe a person led along by the emotion of the moment. Paul compares people who are weak in their faith to children who are

"tossed to and fro and carried about with every wind of doctrine, by the trickery of men, in the cunning craftiness of deceitful plotting" (Ephesians 4:14). When we allow our moods to manage us, instead of the other way around, we give anyone the power to manipulate us! But when we strengthen our faith, we can stand firm in God's promises.

5. "Since we have a great High Priest who has entered heaven, Jesus the Son of God, let us hold firmly to what we believe. This High Priest of ours understands our weaknesses, for he faced all of the same testings we do, yet he did not sin" (Hebrews 4:14–15 NLT). Jesus knows all about mood swings, cravings, disappointments, and embarrassment. He understands sadness, mixed feelings, misgivings, and relief. The writer of Hebrews says Jesus understands us so well because He went through it all too. What a relief it is to have a Savior who knows how we feel!

6. "Let the word of Christ dwell in you richly in all wisdom, teaching and admonishing one another in psalms and hymns and spiritual songs, singing with grace in your hearts to the Lord" (Colossians 3:16). Don't be ruled by your present mood. Instead, let your heart be ruled by Scripture—the Word of Christ dwelling in you! When we heed Jesus' words, we are filled with His wisdom and peace. We'll be able to reach out to others who are struggling and encourage them, and our hearts will be filled with praise and thanksgiving. When Scripture is firmly planted in our hearts, we cannot be manipulated by our own emotions.

SESSION 2

1. "The heart is deceitful above all things, And desperately wicked; Who can know it?" (Jeremiah 17:9). Selfishness is deeply rooted in our hearts. It dictates our decisions, our first impulses, and our gut reactions. Our hearts are deceitful—easily wooed away from what is right and good. Even after we have given our hearts to God, our desires can betray us and lead us into sin.

2. "He who trusts in his own heart is a fool, But whoever walks wisely will be delivered" (Proverbs 28:26). We are fools if we follow our hearts and our hearts alone. We have to engage our brains and balance our hearts with our heads. True happiness comes from walking down the path God has created for us.

3. "Take heed to yourselves, lest your heart be deceived, and you turn aside and serve other gods and worship them" (Deuteronomy 11:16). God wants us to be on guard. Our hearts can be deceived, so we must protect them. We should be serving Him, not chasing the fleeting pleasures of this world.

4. "Trust in the LORD with all your heart, And lean not on your own understanding" (Proverbs 3:5). God is upfront with us. He tells us outright how we can't trust our emotions. Instead, He pleads with us to put our trust in Him. Take Him at His word. Believe Him, and act on what He asks of you.

5. "The LORD is near to those who have a broken heart, And saves such as have a contrite spirit" (Psalm 34:18). God is able to help us, but only if we give up control and come to Him with brokenness—admitting our inability to help ourselves, confessing our failings, and submitting to His guidance.

6. "I will give you a new heart and put a new spirit within you; I will take the heart of stone out of your flesh and give you a heart of flesh" (Ezekiel 36:26). Even though our hearts are hard, deceitful, and selfish, God is able to give us a new heart that longs to follow after Him.

SESSION 3

1. "An angry man stirs up strife, And a furious man abounds in transgression" (Proverbs 29:22). When we let our anger get the better of us, we behave badly, and our sins start to pile up. Anger never solves anything; it only leads to more problems.

2. "People with understanding control their anger; a hot temper shows great foolishness" (Proverbs 14:29 NLT). Perhaps the first step in controlling our tempers is understanding the things that set us off. If we can anticipate our anger, we'll be less likely to say or do something foolish that we'll later regret.

3. Jonah tells God, "It is right for me to be angry, even to death!" (Jonah 4:9). But instead of reacting with His own wrath, God deals patiently with Jonah while still showing him the error of his ways. Thank goodness we have a God who loves us, even in our worst moments.

4. Psalm 37:8 says "Cease from anger, and forsake wrath." Cease and forsake. Not only should we stop being angry, we should renounce it entirely. Ephesians 4:31 tells us to "Let all bitterness, wrath, anger, clamor, and evil speaking be put away from you, with all malice." *Put them away from you.* And in Colossians 3:8, Paul says to "put off all these: anger, wrath, malice, blasphemy, filthy language." Other translations use words like "stop," "turn," "don't," "bridle," "make a clean break," "get rid of," and "put these things out of your life."

5. We can't pretend we don't get angry. We can't suppress the emotion and deny its existence. But the Bible helps us. "Don't sin by letting anger control you. Think about it overnight and remain silent" (Psalm 4:4 NLT). There are times when anger is justified. There are times when anger is the right reaction in a situation. It's only when we let our anger control us that it leads us into sin. Rather than venting, keep your cool and think things over before you speak.

6. "He who is slow to anger is better than the mighty, And he who rules his spirit than he who takes a city" (Proverbs 16:32). When you are working to manage your emotions, you can detect the beginnings of anger. Then you can search out your motives, watch your reactions, and slow down the rush toward an explosion. With God's help, we won't be at the mercy of a quick temper.

SESSION 4

1. Let's compare different translations of this passage. They're all just a little different. "A sound heart is life to the body, But envy is rottenness to the bones" (Proverbs 14:30). "A peaceful heart leads to a healthy body; jealousy is like cancer in the bones" (NLT). "Peace of mind means a healthy body, but jealousy will rot your bones" (NCV). "A sound mind makes for a robust body, but runaway emotions corrode the bones" (MSG). No matter what translation you use, it's clear that jealousy is toxic!

2. "He who is greedy for gain troubles his own house, But he who hates bribes will live" (Proverbs 15:27). When we get greedy and envious of what others have, we only add to our troubles and strife. Instead of being tempted by the material things of this world, we should remember that God will always see to our needs.

3. "Incline my heart to Your testimonies, And not to covetousness" (Psalm 119:36). Don't let envy dictate your actions. Don't do something just to keep up with the Joneses. Don't adjust your standards to fit the current levels of social acceptability. The psalmist says our hearts should lean towards God's Word, and that should dictate our actions.

4. Paul said in 1 Corinthians 10:24, "Let no one seek his own, but each one the other's well-being." And Philippians 2:4 reads, "Let each of you look out not only for his own interests, but also for the interests

of others." Instead of focusing on what other people have, we should focus on what other people *don't* have. There is always someone in the world who is less fortunate than you are. We can guard against our own jealousy by working to meet the needs of others.

5. "Martha was distracted by the big dinner she was preparing. She came to Jesus and said, 'Lord, doesn't it seem unfair to you that my sister just sits here while I do all the work? Tell her to come and help me'" (Luke 10:40 NLT). There's our childish human impulse again, to complain that "It's not fair!" But Jesus says, "My dear Martha, you are worried and upset over all these details! There is only one thing worth being concerned about. Mary has discovered it—and it will not be taken away from her" (Luke 10:41–42 NLT). Like Martha, we need to look up from our busywork, let go of our resentment, and study the bigger picture. As Jesus Himself said, it's the only thing worth being concerned about!

6. "Make a careful exploration of who you are and the work you have been given, and then sink yourself into that. Don't be impressed with yourself. Don't compare yourself with others. Each of you must take responsibility for doing the creative best you can with your own life" (Galatians 6:4–5 MSG). Search out your own heart and. examine the motivation behind your actions. Are you working for the Lord, or are you trying to compete? Remember, in the end you won't have to answer for anyone but yourself. Put God before everything else and give Him your best.

7. "Now he who plants and he who waters are one, and each one will receive his own reward according to his own labor" (1 Corinthians 3:8). We're all equal in God's eyes. He has no partiality. He plays no favorites. The Lord will be just in rewarding each of us according to our faithfulness, so we shouldn't compare ourselves with others. We know things will be fair in the end.

SESSION 5

1. "Reproach has broken my heart, And I am full of heaviness; I looked for someone to take pity, but there was none; And for comforters, but I found none" (Psalm 69:20). David feels like an outsider, an outcast. He has no one to tell his troubles to. If he had someone there to listen to his sorrows, to comfort him in his sadness, things would feel very different. But David is alone, and that's how he feels: alone.

2. Throughout his travels, Paul experienced many hardships, and not all of them were physical. Even though he had many friends, traveled with several companions, and was close to God, Paul knew loneliness. Paul wasn't somehow exempt. Even the "greatest" of Christians has these kinds of feelings. We all do.

3. "Two people are better off than one, for they can help each other succeed. If one person falls, the other can reach out and help. But someone who falls alone is in real trouble. Likewise, two people lying close together can keep each other warm. But how can one be warm alone?" (Ecclesiastes 4:9–11 NLT). Maybe it's a spouse, a family member, or a good friend, but we've all had the experience of someone being there to help us when we needed it. What a difference it makes when someone is there to carry the load!

4. "Now she who is really a widow, and left alone, trusts in God and continues in supplications and prayers night and day" (1 Timothy

5:5). Many of us spend most of our time alone, whether we're widows like Paul mentions, or single, or we don't have close friends, or the only people we see all day are toddlers. Whatever the case may be, it can be especially hard to stave off loneliness when we spend a good chunk of time by ourselves. When there is no one to talk to, we must turn to God. Paul says our option is to trust Him and to pray. When there's no one else to listen, He will.

5. "Trust in Him at all times, you people; Pour out your heart before Him; God is a refuge for us" (Psalm 62:8). You are not left alone. God is your refuge from loneliness, and He welcomes us to pour out our hearts before Him.

6. In John 16:32 Jesus says, "Indeed the hour is coming, yes, has now come, that you will be scattered, each to his own, and will leave Me alone. And yet I am not alone, because the Father is with Me." Jesus didn't worry about His friends abandoning Him, for He knew God was always with Him. As much as we try to avoid loneliness and surround ourselves with friends, there will be times when no one is around. Yet even in those moments, we are never really alone, because our heavenly Father is with us.

SESSION 6

1. "Search me, O God, and know my heart; Try me, and know my anxieties" (Psalm 139:23). The God who knows our hearts so well understands we get worried. He sees everything, so we don't have to feel embarrassed or ashamed to bring our fears and anxieties to Him.

2. "Whenever I am afraid, I will trust in You" (Psalm 56:3). Notice how David says, "whenever." He doesn't deny the fact he's been afraid, and he knows fear will strike his heart again. God doesn't say He will protect us from being afraid, but He promises that when we are fearful, we can put our faith in Him.

3. Psalm 91:5 tells us, "You shall not be afraid of the terror by night, Nor of the arrow that flies by day." In other words, we don't need to be afraid of the things that go bump in the night—figments of our imagination and borrowed troubles. We don't need to worry about the dangers and troubles our day might hold. And Psalm 112:7 assures us that we don't need to worry about bad news, for God will be with us in our hour of need: "He will not be afraid of evil tidings; His heart is steadfast, trusting in the LORD."

4. "In God (I will praise His word), In God I have put my trust; I will not fear. What can flesh do to me?" (Psalm 56:4). No matter what might come—struggles, disease, conflict, death—none of it can

really touch the part of us that will live forever. This life, with all its worries, is only temporary. We must remember it will pass. Keep trusting God.

5. "That is why I tell you not to worry about everyday life—whether you have enough food and drink, or enough clothes to wear. Isn't life more than food, and your body more than clothing? Look at the birds. They don't plant or harvest or store food in barns, for your heavenly Father feeds them. And aren't you far more valuable to him than they are? Can all your worries add a single moment to your life?" (Matthew 6:25–27 NLT). God's got our necessities covered. After all, He takes care of the plants and animals, and we're far more precious to Him than they are! It doesn't do us any good to worry about our everyday lives; we'll be much better off when we turn our troubles over to God.

6. "Peace I leave with you, My peace I give to you; not as the world gives do I give to you. Let not your heart be troubled, neither let it be afraid" (John 14:27). Whatever you may be facing, set aside your worries and fears and accept Jesus' gift of peace.

SESSION 7

1. "I'm tired of all this—so tired. My bed has been floating forty days and nights on the flood of my tears. My mattress is soaked, soggy with tears" (Psalm 6:6 MSG). David knew how it felt to be so tired that he couldn't go on. And he wasn't just having a bad day; he was plagued by the blues for forty days and nights.

2. "A merry heart does good, like medicine, But a broken spirit dries the bones" (Proverbs 17:22). The *New Living Translation* says, "A broken spirit saps a person's strength." If you're experiencing spiritual listlessness, it could be because some recent experience left you drained. Take the time to rest and restore yourself in Christ, and He will grant you a merry heart.

3. "For the hearts of this people have grown dull. Their ears are hard of hearing, And their eyes they have closed, Lest they should see with their eyes and hear with their ears, Lest they should understand with their hearts and turn, So that I should heal them" (Acts 28:27). Sometimes, we know we are doing wrong, but we'd rather not change. So we shut our ears and shut our eyes to the truth, to the Spirit, and in so doing, we become dull.

4. "Meanwhile, the moment we get tired in the waiting, God's Spirit is right alongside helping us along. If we don't know how or what to pray, it doesn't matter. He does our praying in and for us, making

prayer out of our wordless sighs, our aching groans" (Romans 8:26 MSG). The Holy Spirit stays with us through periods of waiting and helps us to pray in the midst of them. He communicates our feelings to God when we can't find the words to describe them.

5. "Come to Me, all you who labor and are heavy laden, and I will give you rest. Take My yoke upon you and learn from Me, for I am gentle and lowly in heart, and you will find rest for your souls. For My yoke is easy and My burden is light" (Matthew 11:28–30). When we are tired and feeling weighed down, Jesus offers us rest for our weary souls. We can give Him our troubles and heaviness, and in return He will give us His peaceful and gentle Spirit.

6. "I would have lost heart, unless I had believed That I would see the goodness of the Lord In the land of the living" (Psalm 27:13). Waiting will not last forever. No matter how long you've been drifting in the doldrums, never lose faith that God will send you a fresh breeze.

SESSION 8

1. "My heart is in turmoil and cannot rest; Days of affliction confront me" (Job 30:27). This is exactly how it feels our days and emotions are scattered; we're in turmoil, unable to get the rest and peace we so desperately need.

2. "I am feeble and severely broken; I groan because of the turmoil of my heart (Psalm 38:8). When we're scattered in too many directions and overwhelmed by it all, we feel weak, even broken. Our hearts are troubled, which only leads us to feel even more scattered and overwhelmed.

3. "A prayer of the afflicted, when he is overwhelmed and pours out his complaint before the LORD. Hear my prayer, O LORD, And let my cry come to You" (Psalm 102:1). David turned to God when he was over-whelmed. He prayed to the Lord and poured out his heart to Him when he had nowhere else to turn.

4. "From the end of the earth I will cry to You, When my heart is over-whelmed; Lead me to the rock that is higher than I" (Psalm 61:2). We don't have to try to pull ourselves together before facing our Lord. We can cry out to Him from our place of brokenness, and God will hear our call. David asks God to lead him to the rock that is higher. We need something more, something greater, something stronger than ourselves when we are overwhelmed. We need God.

5. "Teach me Your way, O LORD; I will walk in Your truth; Unite my heart to fear Your name" (Psalm 86:11). What an perfect choice of words! I love the contrast between how scattered our hearts and feelings can become and David's plea for God to unite his heart. When we follow God's example and walk in His truth, that is exactly what happens.

6. "Blessed is the man whose strength is in You, Whose heart is set on pilgrimage" (Psalm 84:5). When we talk about staying focused and having purpose, we can think of David's psalm here. We need to rely on God to give us strength and set our hearts on the path He wants us to pursue, no matter what distractions try to lure us off track.

SESSION 9

1. "The foolishness of a man twists his way, And his heart frets against the Lord" (Proverbs 19:3). When we push ourselves away from what the Lord asks us to do, we're being foolish. We know in our heart of hearts that God's way is good. But we also know His way isn't always easy. Resisting a change can have serious consequences. *The Message* is predictably blunt: "People ruin their lives by their own stupidity, so why does God always get blamed?"

2. "Those who are of a perverse heart are an abomination to the Lord, But the blameless in their ways are His delight" (Proverbs 11:20). In other words, "God can't stand deceivers" (msg). As much as we may want to hold on to our contrariness, it is a relief to let go of our rebellion and accept God's Word. And this proverb gives us all the motivation we need to do so; none of us wants to be an abomination to the Lord.

3. "This perverse way of life will be like a towering, badly built wall that slowly, slowly tilts and shifts, and then one day, without warning, collapses" (Isaiah 30:13 msg). The reality of living contrary to God is that we are fooling ourselves. We think what we are building is fine and beautiful and satisfying, but in reality it is like a house of cards, doomed to fall. One day, God will force us to face the truth, and the reality check will leave us stunned. We will regret the time we wasted in worthless pursuits, the lost opportunities to give glory to God,

and the painful consequences of our perversity. Perhaps then, we will wish we had been more receptive, more teachable, less stubborn, and less determined to go our own way.

4. "In accordance with your hardness and your impenitent heart you are treasuring up for yourself wrath in the day of wrath and revelation of the righteous judgment of God" (Romans 2:5). We look around and see all kinds of sin in the world. It's socially acceptable to do all manner of wickedness, and most people don't care what God's perspective might be. When we harbor sin in our contrary moods, we're just as bad as the rest of the world. Don't cling to things with an unrepentant heart. Don't let hardness prevent you from hearing the Spirit's quiet urging. Such behavior only stirs up God's wrath against sin.

5. "See, O LORD, that I am in distress; My soul is troubled; My heart is overturned within me, For I have been very rebellious" (Lamentations 1:20). When we recognize the rebellious streak in our hearts, the Holy Spirit urges us to be honest before the Lord. After all, He is the only one who can help us!

6. "Since we respect our earthly fathers who disciplined us, shouldn't we submit even more to the discipline of the Father of our spirits, and live forever?" (Hebrews 12:9 NLT). We need to trust our Heavenly Father and submit ourselves cheerfully to His will. When we do, He will bestow to us all His wonderful blessings, including eternal life.

SESSION 10

1. As each month passes, we are given a fresh opportunity to show a steadfast spirit. It's so much easier to grouse and sulk and groan, but we don't have to be ruled by our tumbled feelings. God doesn't necessarily ask us to take on great things when we are feeling our weakest, but He gives us the chance to pull through with grace.

2. "Out of the abundance of the heart the mouth speaks. A good man out of the good treasure of his heart brings forth good things, and an evil man out of the evil treasure brings forth evil things" (Matthew 12:34–35). When we say and do things that we are ashamed of later, it reveals the needs in our hearts. When this happens, take the time to make things right with God and with others.

3. "A wise woman strengthens her family, but a foolish woman destroys hers by what she does" (Proverbs 14:1 NCV). We all want to make our families stronger, but when we're in a bad mood we can act foolishly, tearing down the things that we're supposed to build up. Just because we're "not in the mood" to do the right thing doesn't give us the excuse to behave badly. When we do good, in spite of the difficulty, we are wise.

4. A person who has a self-willed heart acts out of purely selfish motives. When considering what to do, their first thoughts are: *What do I want? What would I like? What do I feel like doing?* When a heart is

God-willed, it means that God comes first. Before we act or react, we consider God's wishes in the situation. We act on His behalf, as His servant in all things.

5. Paul wanted to live in such a way that Jesus would be revealed in him. Is that your prayer? Do you want people to look at you and see the changes wrought by Christ? Does your heart, which belongs to Jesus, shine forth to others—even when you're not in the mood?

6. "What does the Lord your God require of you, but to fear the Lord your God, to walk in all His ways and to love Him, to serve the Lord your God with all your heart and with all your soul, and to keep the commandments of the Lord and His statutes which I command you today for your good?" (Deuteronomy 10:12–13). Fearing God means loving Him with all our heart and soul. It also means keeping His commandments and following the path He has laid out for us. No matter what emotional state we're in, we can't let it distract us from this important truth.

SESSION 11

1. Paul describes ungodly people as "hopelessly confused" (Ephesians 4:17 NLT). They have closed their minds and hardened their hearts to God, and don't care about right or wrong. All they care about is what feels good. Paul reminds us we are no longer like this. As Christians, we are to walk away from our former way of life and let the Spirit renew our thoughts and attitudes.

2. "There is a way that seems right to a man, But its end is the way of death" (Proverbs 14:12). Solomon reminds us that we cannot trust our own instincts because our heart is deceitful. But Jesus knows the way we should go. Our Shepherd will lead us onto the right path. All we have to do is follow Him.

3. Isaiah 53:6 says, "We're all like sheep who've wandered off and gotten lost. We've all done our own thing, gone our own way" (MSG). And Jeremiah 50:6 elaborates on this: "My people were lost sheep . . . they wandered aimless through the hills. They lost track of home, couldn't remember where they came from" (MSG). When we try to do things our own way, we lose sight of God and the plans He has for us. We wander away, and sometimes we go so far off the path that we get completely lost.

4. "'I will set up shepherds over them who will feed them; and they shall fear no more, nor be dismayed, nor shall they be lacking,' says

the Lord" (Jeremiah 23:4). Whether we're lost in sin, lost in doubts or fears, or lost in an emotional whirlwind, God will take care of us and send us the help we need.

5. "I myself will be the shepherd of my sheep. I myself will make sure they get plenty of rest. I'll go after the lost, I'll collect the strays, I'll doctor the injured, I'll build up the weak ones and oversee the strong ones so they're not exploited" (Ezekiel 34:15–16 MSG). God sees us when we're tired, lost, and weak, and He won't let us stay that way. He will collect us and bring us back to Him. He will look after us and give us rest from our troubles.

6. "I am the good shepherd; and I know My sheep, and am known by My own. As the Father knows Me, even so I know the Father; and I lay down My life for the sheep" (John 10:14–15). Jesus knows us and wants us to know Him. He loves us so much that He laid down His life to save us, His precious sheep. We can feel safe in following Him because we know He wants the best for us.

7. "You are my rock and my fortress; Therefore, for Your name's sake, Lead me and guide me" (Psalm 31:3). Always, but especially when we're feeling lost or adrift, we can trust Jesus to be our rock. The best thing we can do when we're overwhelmed is to surrender the controls to Him. We can be sure He will lead us on the right path.

SESSION 12

1. "Choose for yourselves this day whom you will serve . . . But as for me and my house, we will serve the LORD" (Joshua 24:15). When we face our options and deliberately place ourselves in the Lord's service, we know that we are doing the right thing.

2. "Depend on the LORD and His strength; always go to Him for help" (Psalm 105:4 NCV). We often don't have enough willpower to resist our sinful inclinations or keep our emotions in check. Luckily for us, God is an everlasting source of strength. It is to Him we should turn. It is upon Him we must depend.

3. "That Christ may dwell in your hearts through faith; that you, being rooted and grounded in love, may be able to comprehend with all the saints what is the width and length and depth and height—to know the love of Christ which passes knowledge; that you may be filled with all the fullness of God" (Ephesians 3:17–19). At times our muddled feelings can get in our way, but it's very important for us to experience emotions. How could God's people understand a God who is love, if we could not feel love? We have these emotions because God made us a little like Himself. We feel because He feels.

4. "As each one has received a gift, minister it to one another, as good stewards of the manifold grace of God" (1 Peter 4:10). Since our emotions are gifts from God, we must manage them as well as we can.

When we are good stewards of our emotions, we can use them to help other people and to bring glory to God.

5. Isaiah tells us we must "learn to do good" (Isaiah 1:17). No matter what's going on in our hearts on a given day, doing good must become our way of life. Hebrews 13:16 advises us, "Do not forget to do good and to share, for with such sacrifices God is well pleased." God knows doing good is not easy for us; that's why He considers it a sacrifice. We have the opportunity to make a beautiful, loving sacrifice each and every day!

6. "Let us not grow weary while doing good, for in due season we shall reap if we do not lose heart" (Galatians 6:9). Even if you're never able to manage yourself perfectly, don't lose heart. Doing good is the noblest pursuit we can have, one that will pay dividends both in this life and the next.